NATIONAL GEOGRAPHIC

Ladders

T0288431

Living
IN THE
MOUNTAINS
Communities We Live In

2 **Tall Mountains, Big Goals** *Narrative*
by Debbie Nevins and Ann Wildman

10 **Surfing the Snowy Mountains** *Reference Article*
by Sean O'Shea

16 **Comparing Mountain Communities** *Comparison Article*
by Annaliese Toth

24 **Discuss**

TALL MOUNTAINS,

Jordan Romero stood on the top of Vinson Massif. This is the highest mountain in Antarctica. "We made it!" he shouted. It was December 24, 2011, and Jordan had reached his **goal**. He had climbed the highest mountain on every **continent**. A continent is a large landmass on Earth.

Jordan had set this goal when he was 10. He saw a mural showing the **summits**, or tops, of the highest mountains on the seven continents. Jordan thought, "I'd like to climb these mountains!" But he couldn't

∧ Climbing rope

< Jordan stands between his stepmom on the left and his dad on the right. They are at the top of Vinson Massif.

2

Big Goals

by Debbie Nevins
and Ann Wildman

start just yet. Jordan and his dad had to get permission from each country. They needed the right gear. And Jordan had to start training. Jordan was living in a mountain community in California. He was used to running and climbing in the mountains. But he would have to do special training to meet such a big goal.

⌃ Vinson Massif is located in Antarctica.
It was discovered in 1935.

The Seven Summits

Jordan and his dad began hiking in the Sierra Nevada, a mountain range. Jordan carried a heavy backpack. This helped build his strength. He ran in the mountains. This helped him learn to breathe at high **elevations**. Elevation is the height of a mountaintop above sea level, or the surface of the sea. It is harder to breathe at higher elevations. Higher elevations can cause people

Follow along as Jordan and his team climb the "Seven Summits."

SUMMIT 4
Mount Aconcagua
(ah-kawng-KAH-gwah)
in South America
22,841 feet

JORDAN'S CLIMB
December 2007, age 11

This mountain had very strong winds. Only Jordan, his dad, and his stepmom made it to the summit.

SUMMIT 3
Mount Elbrus
in Europe
18,510 feet

JORDAN'S CLIMB
July 2007, age 10

The high elevations made Jordan's dad sick. He felt weak and his head hurt. That's when Jordan took the lead.

SUMMIT 5
Mount McKinley
in North America
20,320 feet

JORDAN'S CLIMB
June 2008, age 11

This mountain's summit was snowy. Jordan had to use the right gear so he didn't slip off the side.

SUMMIT 7
Vinson Massif
in Antarctica
16,067 feet

JORDAN'S CLIMB
December 2011, age 15

Jordan achieved his Seven Summit goal. He climbed this mountain in the summer. But it was still very cold.

to feel sick. This is called elevation sickness. Jordan worked hard for months. He was finally ready to start climbing the highest mountain on each continent.

Jordan celebrates a successful climb in New Guinea.

SUMMIT 6
Mount Everest
in Asia
29,023 feet

JORDAN'S CLIMB
May 2010, age 13

Jordan became the youngest person to climb Everest. He climbed parts of the mountain for weeks. This helped him get used to the elevation.

SUMMIT 2
Mount Kosciuszko
(kosh-CHOOSH-ko)
in Australia
7,310 feet

JORDAN'S CLIMB
April 2007, age 10

This is a smaller mountain. Jordan thought it would be easy to climb. But cold temperatures, rain, and wind slowed him down.

SUMMIT 1
Mount Kilimanjaro
(kil-uh-muhn-JAHR-oh)
in Africa
19,340 feet

JORDAN'S CLIMB
July 2006, age 10

Kilimanjaro has warm rain forests, hard lava, and even snow and ice!

BONUS CLIMB
Carstensz Pyramid
(KAR-stunz)
in New Guinea
16,023 feet

JORDAN'S CLIMB
September 2009, age 13

Some people think Carstensz Pyramid is part of the Seven Summits instead of Mount Kosciuszko.

Jordan's Most Challenging Summit

Jordan worked hard to climb each mountain. But Mount Everest in Asia was his biggest challenge. It is the highest mountain in the world. Climbers face freezing temperatures and strong winds. Avalanches, or sliding ice and snow, hurt climbers every year.

Jordan was not afraid of these dangers. He was with his trusted team—his dad, stepmom, and three *Sherpas*. Sherpas are skilled climbers who live near the mountain. Jordan's team had warm clothing and special boots that helped them stay on the ice. Hooks, ropes, tools, tents, and oxygen all helped them reach the summit. Still, the journey was tiring. At times, Jordan's legs felt as heavy as cement.

Jordan kept climbing. He was determined to reach his goal. Jordan explains how he felt at the summit of Mount Everest. "It was the best 20 minutes of my life, seeing the curve of the Earth and the endless miles." He couldn't stay for too long, though. It is very cold on top of Mount Everest. But before Jordan started to climb down, he called his mom.

"Mom," he said, "I'm calling you from the top of the world."

Jordan (right) and a Sherpa guide wear masks during their climb. The masks help them breathe the thin mountain air.

Yes, that's Jordan buried under all of that warm clothing. It protects him from the weather as he climbs Mount Everest.

Getting to Know Jordan

For Jordan, every day is an adventure. He sets big goals and works hard to achieve them. Let's get to know Jordan a little better.

National Geographic: How did you get interested in mountain climbing?

Jordan Romero: I originally got outdoors to see nature. I really liked animals, especially snakes. Then it was watching films about the big mountain peaks on Discovery Channel and National Geographic that really sparked my interest for climbing.

NG: Did you do anything unusual to train for a big climb?

JR: For some climbs we have to pull sleds full of gear up the mountain. So I tied a tire to my waist and dragged it behind me to practice pulling the weight.

NG: Were you scared while climbing Mount Everest?

JR: On day 17, Dad and I got swept up in an avalanche, and Dad got a bit hurt. It scared me for a day or so, then we got back on-mission.

NG: Did you have to do schoolwork on each of your climbs?

JR: I had to travel with all my studies and books, and I was doing algebra on Mount Everest. It was hard doing homework on climbs, but it had to get done.

NG: How was climbing Mount Everest with your family?

JR: It was the time of my life. They put it all on the line for me. I'm grateful for their support.

NG: What are your current goals?

JR: I'd like to complete the Adventure Grand Slam. This involves climbing the Seven Summits (done!) and trekking to the North and South Poles. My mom and I are also planning to help build a school in Malawi, a country in Africa.

Jordan stays safe by using ropes. He attaches the ropes to himself and to the mountain. They will catch him if he stumbles.

Jordan, 14, leads a blind climber to the summit of Quandary Peak in Colorado.

Check In What mountain do you think was the hardest for Jordan to climb? Why?

9

Surfing the Snowy Mountains

by Sean O'Shea

A snowboarder spins and swirls over the snow.

Imagine zipping down a snowy mountain. Your boots are clipped to a snowboard. That's a short, wide ski. You hit a snowdrift and fly into the air. Hold on!

If you've ever gone skateboarding, you might know what snowboarding is like. You stand on the board in much the same way. You bend your knees and balance. But you're not on the sidewalk. You're on a snowy slope.

Some boarders like to swoosh back and forth in a **bowl**. A bowl is a curved area of snow. Think of a big scoop taken out of the ground. Then add snow. Mountain communities have curved bowls, steep slopes, and thick snow. They are a perfect place to snowboard.

How Snowboarding Became a Sport

1963
Seventh grader Tom Sims builds a "ski board." He wants a way to skateboard in the snow.

1970s
Early snowboarders make their own snowboards. Their designs become popular. Several companies begin to make them.

1980s
Snowboarders begin to get together for contests around the world.

1998
Snowboarding becomes a sport in the Winter Olympic Games. The Olympics at Nagano, Japan, are the first to include snowboarding events.

2000
Snowboarding becomes the fastest-growing sport in the United States.

Gearing Up

Snowboarding is a challenging sport. It can also be dangerous. A snowboarder has to make quick decisions to stay safe. It takes years of training and hard work to become a snowboarding **athlete**. Let's look at the gear snowboarders use.

Snowboards are five to six feet long. Most snowboards are about ten inches wide. They come in many shapes and sizes. Different snowboards help you do different tricks. They also help you control your speed and make turns.

Boots and bindings attach to your feet. They keep you on the board.

A helmet protects your head. It also keeps your head warm.

Goggles protect your eyes from snow, ice, wind, and sunlight.

Warm jackets and snow pants keep you warm and dry. Snowboarders need to be able to move freely in their clothing.

Gloves with padding protect your hands when you steer. That's important because boarders steer by dragging one hand along the snowy ground.

A leash keeps the board from sliding away if you fall.

Crust-Bustin' Moves

Method Air
Bend your knees while you're in the air. Bring the board behind you and grab it with one hand.

McTwist
Twist around twice as you flip in the air. Skateboarder Mike McGill invented this trick. Others have made it even harder!

180 Grind
Turn halfway around as you jump onto the rail. The rail can be a stairway rail or a small wall. Then turn back at the end of the rail. You should finish facing the same side you started.

Giants of the Slopes

Shaun White

These are three of the many snowboarding champions.

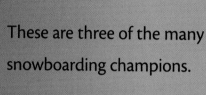

Shaun White is called the "Flying Tomato." His red hair and snowboard tricks earned him that name. Shaun won his first competition at age seven. He has also won two Olympic medals. He did the "double McTwist 1260" at the 2010 games. He flipped twice while doing three-and-a-half spins!

> Shaun White catches some air at a competition in Colorado.

Travis Rice

^ Travis Rice launches off a hill in Colorado.

Travis Rice grew up on the slopes in the state of Wyoming. Travis is a snowboard **freestyle** champion. A freestyle snowboarder performs tricks in a U-shaped ramp. Travis likes to do high jumps. He has even done snowboarding stunts in movies.

Kelly Clark grew up in the state of Vermont near steep, snowy mountains. She has won more snowboarding medals than any other female athlete. In 2011, she did a 1080, or three turns in the air. This was a first for any woman!

Kelly Clark competes in a half-pipe event in New York State.

Kelly Clark

Check In Describe your favorite snowboarder or snowboarding move.

Read to find out about two mountain communities in different parts of the world.

Comparing Mountain Communities

by Annaliese Toth

Two Locations

Mountain communities are in every corner of the world. Let's compare two communities in different countries.

CRESTED BUTTE The Rocky Mountains are in North America. Crested Butte (BEWT), Colorado, is in a valley in the Rockies. A valley is low ground between mountains. But the elevation of Crested Butte is still 8,885 feet above sea level. It can get snow as early as September and as late as June. It is about 70°F in summer.

KATHMANDU The Himalaya Mountains stretch across South Asia. They include the country of Nepal. Kathmandu (kat-man-DOO) is the capital city of Nepal. It is in a river valley. Kathmandu is about 4,344 feet above sea level. This lower elevation gives Kathmandu a mild climate. Summer temperatures are about 77°F. Winter temperatures don't get very cold. Snow hardly ever falls in the city.

Populations

CRESTED BUTTE Crested Butte is a small, **rural** community. It doesn't even have a traffic light. About 1,500 people live there. That is its **population**. People living in Crested Butte must go to nearby communities for things they need. For many years, students even traveled to a nearby community to go to high school.

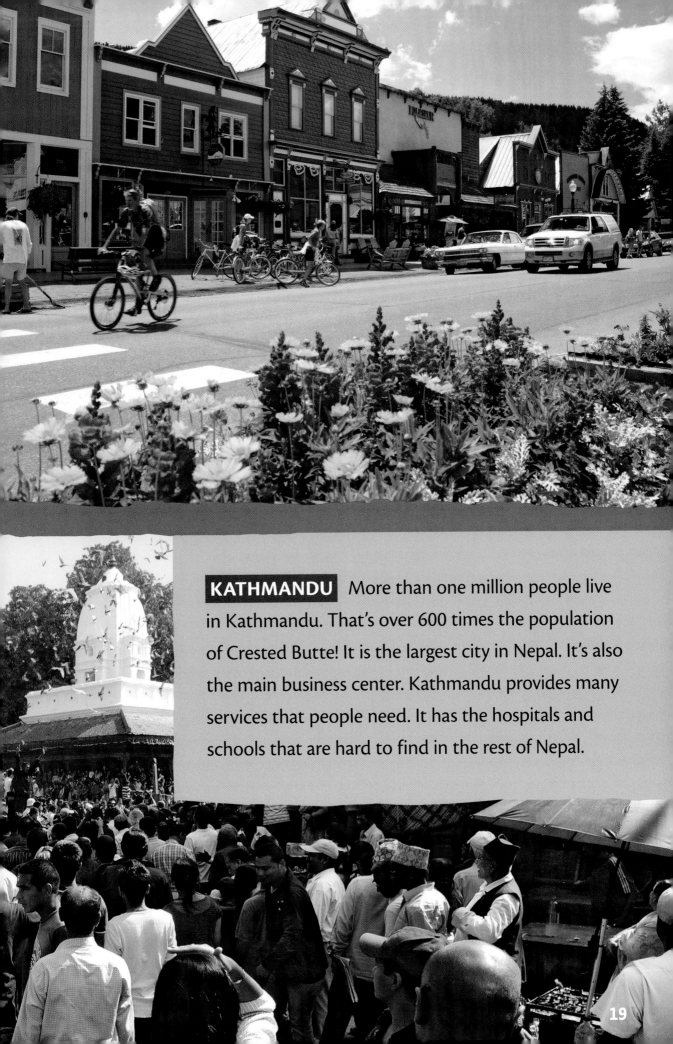

KATHMANDU More than one million people live in Kathmandu. That's over 600 times the population of Crested Butte! It is the largest city in Nepal. It's also the main business center. Kathmandu provides many services that people need. It has the hospitals and schools that are hard to find in the rest of Nepal.

19

Resources

CRESTED BUTTE Settlers in the United States traveled west around 1860. Many came to Crested Butte. They came to mine **resources**, such as gold and coal. New businesses opened to serve the miners. Then the gold and coal ran low. Many mines closed. Some settlers tried to earn money by ranching. Others cut down trees and sold the lumber. But people couldn't earn enough money to support their families. They began to move away. The population of Crested Butte had gone down by the 1950s.

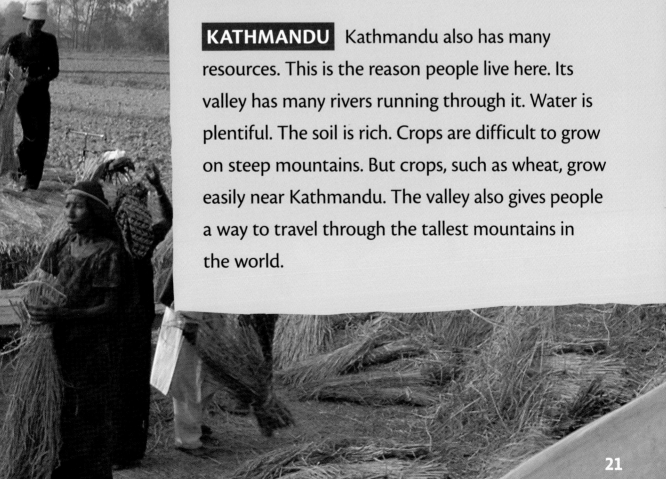

KATHMANDU Kathmandu also has many
resources. This is the reason people live here. Its
valley has many rivers running through it. Water is
plentiful. The soil is rich. Crops are difficult to grow
on steep mountains. But crops, such as wheat, grow
easily near Kathmandu. The valley also gives people
a way to travel through the tallest mountains in
the world.

Populations

CRESTED BUTTE The Rocky Mountain trails near Crested Butte are fun to explore in the summer. Snowy mountains are full of snowboarders and skiers in the winter. Hotels and restaurants welcome tourists, or visitors to the community. Most people who live and work in Crested Butte have jobs helping tourists. Others work in the mountains. They remove snow from roads and keep trails safe.

KATHMANDU Many tourists who plan to climb in the Himalaya Mountains start in Kathmandu. In 1953, the first climbers reached the summit of nearby Mount Everest. Since then, stores, restaurants, and hotels have opened in Kathmandu to serve tourists.

All mountain communities are different. But they all have mountains in common!

Check In How are Crested Butte and Kathmandu similar?

Discuss

1. What do you think connects the three selections that you read in this book? What makes you think that?

2. If you lived in or visited a mountain community, what kinds of goals could you set for yourself? Why?

3. What kinds of activities can you do to have fun in the mountains?

4. What is similar about the community you live in and mountain communities like Crested Butte and Kathmandu? What is different?

5. What do you still wonder about living in the mountains?